D0846020

Team Spirit ®

THE COLORADO AVALANCHE

BY

MARK STEWART

Content Consultant
Denis Gibbons
Society for International Hockey Research

NORWOODHOUSE PRESS

CHICAGO, ILLINOIS

Norwood House Press
P.O. Box 316598
Chicago, Illinois 60631

For information regarding Norwood House Press, please visit our website at:
www.norwoodhousepress.com or call 866-565-2900.

PHOTO CREDITS:
All photos courtesy Getty Images except the following:
World Hockey Association (6), Topps, Inc. (14, 23, 38, 40 bottom),
Esso/Imperial Oil Ltd. (21), O-Pee-Chee Ltd. (29, 37), Tag Express (34),
Classic Games (40 top), The Sporting News (41 top), The National Hockey
League (41 left), Pinnacle Brands (43).
Cover photo: Bill Wippert/Getty Images
Special thanks to Topps, Inc.

Editor: Mike Kennedy
Designer: Ron Jaffe
Project Management: Black Book Partners, LLC.
Research: Joshua Zaffos
Special thanks to Karen Shannon

LIBRARY OF CONGRESS CATALOGING-IN-PUBLICATION DATA

Stewart, Mark, 1960-
  The Colorado Avalanche / By Mark Stewart.
    p. cm. -- (Team spirit)
  Includes bibliographical references and index.
  Summary: "Presents the history and accomplishments of the Colorado
Avalanche hockey team. Includes highlights of players, coaches, and awards,
quotes, timeline, maps, glossary, and websites"--Provided by publisher.
  ISBN-13: 978-1-59953-400-8 (library edition : alk. paper)
  ISBN-10: 1-59953-400-2 (library edition : alk. paper)
  1. Colorado Avalanche (Hockey team)--History--Juvenile literature. 2.
Hockey teams--Colorado--History--Juvenile literature. I. Title.
  GV848.C65S84 2011
  796.962'640978883--dc22
                                        2010010629

Manufactured in the United States of America in North Mankato, Minnesota.
159N—072010

COVER PHOTO: The Avalanche celebrate a victory during the 2009–10 season.

Table of Contents

SPORTS WORDS & VOCABULARY WORDS: In this book, you will find many words that are new to you. You may also see familiar words used in new ways. The glossary on page 46 gives the meanings of hockey words, as well as "everyday" words that have special hockey meanings. These words appear in **bold type** throughout the book. The glossary on page 47 gives the meanings of vocabulary words that are not related to hockey. They appear in ***bold italic type*** throughout the book.

Meet the
Avalanche

Few things in nature are as powerful as an avalanche. When a wall of snow comes tumbling down a mountain, nothing on earth can stop it. From the moment the **National Hockey League (NHL)** agreed to move a team near the mountains of Colorado in 1995, the Avalanche began living up to their name. They have played winning hockey ever since.

The Avalanche began their hockey journey in the 1970s in Canada as the Quebec Nordiques. In both locations, the club discovered something everyone knows today—that great players don't have to speak the same language to play great hockey as a team.

This book tells the story of the Avalanche. They started nearly 2,000 miles away from where they play today, in a different country and in a completely different league. Now they play in an arena that is located almost a mile above sea level. When the Avalanche get rolling, there's no stopping them.

Colorado players show great team spirit after a goal during a 2009–10 game.

Way Back When

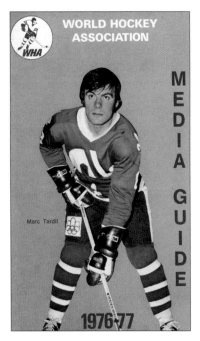

For more than 50 years beginning in 1917, hockey fans had only one major league to follow: the NHL. In 1972, a new league began play to compete with the NHL. It was called the **World Hockey Association (WHA)**. When the WHA formed, it had 12 teams, including the San Francisco Sharks. Before the first season started, the owners moved the Sharks from California to Quebec City in Canada. The team was renamed the Nordiques, which is French for "Northmen." Millions of people speak French in the ***province*** of Quebec.

The WHA was made up of young players hungry for a chance to skate as **professionals**, as well as a few stars who left the NHL to make more money. The first leader of the Nordiques was J.C. Tremblay. He had played in the NHL **All-Star Game** seven times with the Montreal Canadiens. Quebec's young stars in its early years included Rejean Houle, Marc Tardif, Serge Bernier, Christian Bordeleau, Richard Brodeur, Jamie Hislop, and Réal Cloutier. All but Brodeur and Cloutier had seen ice time in the NHL.

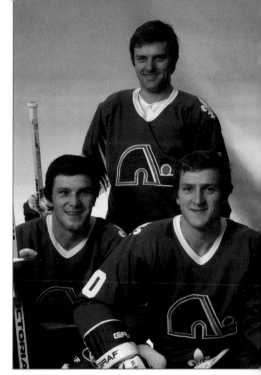

LEFT: Marc Tardif appears on the cover of the WHA's 1976–77 media guide.
RIGHT: Marian Stastny stands behind his brothers Peter and Anton for a photo.

The Nordiques twice played for the WHA championship. They lost in 1974–75 and won in 1976–77. In 1979, the Nordiques were invited to join the NHL, along with three other WHA teams. Facing new competition, a fresh group of stars led the "Nords." One of them was Michel Goulet, who grew up in Quebec. There was also Dale Hunter and the Stastny brothers—Peter, Marian, and Anton. They all helped the team reach the **Eastern Conference Finals** in 1984–85 and earn a **division** championship in 1985–86. Also during this time, the Nordiques had a fierce *rivalry* with the Canadiens, who played just three hours away.

In the early 1990s, Quebec welcomed more young stars, including Joe Sakic, Adam Foote, Owen Nolan, Valeri Kamensky, and Mats Sundin. In 1991, the team **drafted** Eric Lindros, who was expected to be hockey's next superstar. Lindros did not want to play for the Nordiques, so they traded him for a package of talented players that included future stars Peter Forsberg and Mike Ricci. In one year, the team went from 20 wins to 47!

Despite their success, the Nordiques needed to find a city with more fans. After the 1994–95 season, they moved to Denver, Colorado and were renamed the Avalanche. Many years earlier, an NHL team called the Rockies had played there. The fans were excited to root for their new club.

The "Avs" found success immediately. In 1995–96, they reached the **Stanley Cup Finals**. Sakic and superstar goalie Patrick Roy—who joined the team during the season—led Colorado to a four-game sweep of the Florida Panthers. In 2000–01, the Avs won the **Stanley Cup** again.

Year in and year out, the Avs kept winning games and bringing exciting new players to the ice. Some were already stars when they joined the team, including Claude Lemieux, Rob Blake, Sandis Ozolinsh, and Ray Bourque. Others—such as Adam Deadmarsh, Milan Hejduk, Chris Drury, and Alex Tanguay—started their careers with the club. No matter who was wearing the Colorado uniform, they knew what it took to play championship hockey.

LEFT: Joe Sakic, the star forward who led the Avs to two Stanley Cup titles.
RIGHT: Rob Blake, Peter Forsberg, and Patrick Roy

The Team Today

In the years after their 2001 Stanley Cup, the Avalanche continued to bring great players to Colorado. Fans filled the team's arena night after night. They loved hockey and rooting for the Avs.

In 2005, the NHL made new rules that limited the amount of money teams were allowed to spend on player salaries. This created some tough decisions for the Avalanche. In order to keep leaders such as Joe Sakic and Rob Blake in the **lineup**, the team had to part ways with reliable **veterans**, including Peter Forsberg.

Fans hated to see some of their favorite players leave, but they found new stars to support. Newcomers like Paul Stastny, Scott Hannan, Ryan Smyth, Chris Stewart, and Matt Duchene helped the Avalanche have winning seasons and reach the **playoffs**. When Sakic retired in 2009 after 21 years with the team, it marked the end of one amazing *era* and the beginning of another.

Paul Stastny gets words of encouragement from Chris Stewart during a 2009–10 game.

Home Ice

During its years in Canada, the team played in the Quebec Coliseum. It was a huge building that held more than 15,000 fans. When the Avalanche arrived in Colorado in 1995, they played in the McNichols Sports Arena. The "Big Mac" had been home to the Denver Spurs of the WHA in the 1970s. During the 1970s and 1980s, the Colorado Rockies of the NHL also played there.

In 1999, the Avalanche moved into a new arena. It was a big, round building called the Pepsi Center, after the soft drink company. Colorado fans nicknamed it "The Can." In 2008, the arena was home to the ***Democratic National Convention***. During the convention, Barack Obama was officially chosen to run for president.

BY THE NUMBERS

- *There are 18,007 seats for hockey in Colorado's arena.*
- *As of the 2009–10 season, the Avalanche have retired the numbers of three players—Joe Sakic (19), Patrick Roy (33), and Ray Bourque (77).*
- *The Nordiques retired the numbers of four players—J.C. Tremblay (3), Marc Tardif (8), Michel Goulet (16), and Peter Stastny (26).*

The players and fans stand for the national anthem before a 2007–08 game at Colorado's arena.

Dressed for Success

During their 23 seasons in Quebec, the Nordiques wore a blue and white uniform. It included the fleur-de-lis, which is an ancient *symbol* used by French kings and queens. The uniform also had a bright red letter *N* next to a hockey stick. A lot of fans thought it looked like an elephant!

After coming to Colorado, the Avalanche continued to use blue and white as their team colors. They also added black, silver, and a deep red known as burgundy. The Avs wear burgundy uniforms at home and white uniforms on the road.

The team's *logo* features the natural wonders that make Colorado famous, the Rocky Mountains. The logo shows a mountain peak in the shape of the letter *A*, with snow swooshing down behind a hockey puck. The team's uniform has the logo on the front.

JOE SAKIC•C

Joe Sakic models the Quebec uniform from the late 1980s. It features the "red elephant" and the fleur-de-lis.

UNIFORM BASICS

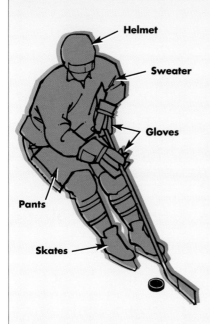

- Helmet
- Sweater
- Gloves
- Pants
- Skates

The hockey uniform has five important parts:
- Helmet
- Sweater
- Pants
- Gloves
- Skates

Hockey helmets are made of hard plastic with softer padding inside. Some players also wear visors to protect their eyes.

The hockey uniform top is called a sweater. Players wear padding underneath it to protect their shoulders, spine and ribs. Padded hockey pants, or "breezers," extend from the waist to the knees. Players also wear padding on their knees and shins.

Hockey gloves protect the top of the hand and the wrist. Only a thin layer of leather covers the palm, which helps a player control his stick. A goalie wears two different gloves—one for catching pucks and one for blocking them. Goalies also wear heavy leg pads and a mask. They paint their masks to match their personalities and team colors.

All players wear hockey skates. The blade is curved at each end. The skate top is made from metal, plastic, nylon, and either real or *synthetic* leather. Goalies wear skates that have extra protection on the toe and ankle.

Goalie Craig Anderson wears the team's 2009–10 home uniform.

We Won!

The Avalanche have won three championships, one in Quebec as the Nordiques and two in Colorado. The first came in 1976–77, when the Nordiques were part of the World Hockey Association. Their top scorers were Réal Cloutier, Marc Tardif, Serge Bernier, and the Bordeleau brothers, Christian and Paulin. The defense was led by J.C. Tremblay and Jim Dorey, and backed by goalie Richard Brodeur.

The Nordiques advanced through the first two rounds of the playoffs. Next, they faced the Winnipeg Jets in the **WHA Finals**. With Tardif and Tremblay slowed by injuries, Bernier stepped up and played like a superstar. The series went the distance. Quebec hosted Game 7 with a chance to win the championship on its home ice. With their fans rooting them on, the Nordiques skated to an 8–2 victory to capture the WHA title.

The team's first NHL championship came right after its move from Quebec to Colorado, in 1995–96. Joe Sakic had a terrific year for the Avalanche. He led the club with 51 goals and 120 points. The team's best **playmaker** was Peter Forsberg, who had 86 **assists**. Colorado had several other top players, including forwards Valeri Kamensky and

Peter Forsberg battles for the puck during the 1995–96 season.

Claude Lemieux, defensemen Uwe Krupp and Sandis Ozolinsh, and goalie Patrick Roy.

The Avalanche faced the Florida Panthers in the Stanley Cup Finals. Colorado took the first three games thanks to the great goaltending of Roy. The Panthers scored just four times in those games. Roy was even better in Game 4. He turned aside shot after shot. But so did Florida goalie John Vanbiesbrouck. Neither team could score in the first 60 minutes. The game remained tied 0–0 after the first **overtime** and then after the second overtime, too.

Finally, in the third overtime, Krupp scored to win the game. Fans were amazed when they saw the stats. The Panthers had fired 63 shots on goal, and Roy had stopped every one. The Conn Smythe Trophy for **Most Valuable Player (MVP)** of the playoffs went to Sakic. He led all players with 18 goals. Six of them were game-winners.

Colorado's second Stanley Cup came five years later. New to the team were forwards Milan Hejduk, Alex Tanguay, and Chris Drury, as well as defensemen Rob Blake and Ray Bourque. They helped the Avalanche produce the best record in the NHL.

Colorado's players and fans desperately wanted Bourque to win a championship. He had played for 21 seasons in the NHL, but the Stanley Cup had always *eluded* him. He joined the Avalanche in 2000, hoping for one last chance at the title.

This time, Colorado's opponent in the finals was the New Jersey Devils. Colorado fans knew it would not be an easy series. The Avs were missing Forsberg, who was out with an injury. The Devils had won the Stanley Cup the year before. Their goalie, Martin Brodeur, was fantastic. Even so, he was not ready for the Avalanche in Game 1. They won 5–0. Sakic skated circles around the New Jersey defense, while Roy was sensational in goal.

The Devils bounced back and took the lead in the series. The Avs traveled to New Jersey for Game 6. The pressure was on Roy and his teammates. They had to win two games in a row to capture the Stanley Cup.

Roy picked the perfect time to be perfect. Nothing the Devils tried in Game 6 worked. Roy stopped 24 shots for a 4–0 victory.

The series moved back to Colorado for Game 7. The Devils kept a close watch on Colorado's top scorers. But Tanguay still found room to skate. The 21-year-old snapped two shots past Brodeur, and Sakic added a third goal. Colorado won 3–1. The Avs were Stanley Cup champions for the second time.

LEFT: The Avs win the 1996 Stanley Cup.   **ABOVE**: Alex Tanguay celebrates a goal during Game 7 against the New Jersey Devils.

Go-To Guys

To be a true star in the NHL, you need more than a great slapshot. You have to be a "go-to guy"—someone teammates trust to make the winning play when the seconds are ticking away in a big game. Fans in Quebec and Colorado have had a lot to cheer about over the years, including these great stars ...

THE PIONEERS

J.C. TREMBLAY   Defenseman

• BORN: 1/22/1939   • DIED: 12/7/1994   • PLAYED FOR TEAM: 1972–73 TO 1978–79

Jean-Claude "J.C." Tremblay was Quebec's first star. During the 1960s, he had been one of the NHL's best defensemen. With the Nordiques, Tremblay was very good at stopping an opponent's top scorers and even better at setting up goals. He led the WHA in assists twice.

MARC TARDIF   Left Wing

• BORN: 6/12/1949   • PLAYED FOR TEAM: 1974–75 TO 1982–83

Marc Tardif won two Stanley Cups with the Montreal Canadiens before jumping to the WHA. He scored 71 goals in his first full season with the Nordiques. He led them to the WHA title one year later.

RÉAL CLOUTIER   Right Wing

• BORN: 7/30/1956 • PLAYED FOR TEAM: 1974–75 TO 1982–83

Réal Cloutier was only 17 when he signed with the Nordiques. At the time, the NHL didn't allow teenagers to play. Cloutier showed he was ready by scoring 86 goals in the WHA before he turned 20.

MICHEL GOULET   Left Wing

• BORN: 4/21/1960 • PLAYED FOR TEAM: 1979–80 TO 1989–90

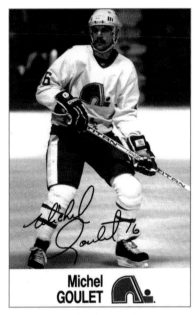

Michel Goulet was a favorite of the French-speaking fans in Quebec. He used his accurate shot to score more than 50 goals four years in a row. After his playing days, Goulet helped *assemble* Colorado's two Stanley Cup champions.

PETER STASTNY   Center

• BORN: 9/18/1956 • PLAYED FOR TEAM: 1980–81 TO 1989–90

Peter Stastny was one of three brothers who played for the Nordiques in the 1980s. He was a swift skater and a *remarkable* scorer. Stastny was the first player in NHL history to score more than 100 points as a **rookie**.

Michel Goulet

ANTON STASTNY   Left Wing

• BORN: 8/5/1959 • PLAYED FOR TEAM: 1980–81 TO 1988–89

Anton Stastny played on the same line with his brother Peter for many years. Anton was an excellent offensive player. He had a goal or an assist in almost every game he played.

JOE SAKIC   Center

• BORN: 7/7/1969 • PLAYED FOR TEAM: 1988–89 TO 2008–09

Joe Sakic became an instant hero in Colorado by leading the team to the Stanley Cup in 1996. "Super Joe" had a hard, accurate wrist shot. He used it to set the Avs' record with 625 goals during his career.

PATRICK ROY   Goalie

• BORN: 10/5/1965 • PLAYED FOR TEAM: 1995–96 TO 2002–03

Patrick Roy won the Conn Smythe Trophy as the MVP of the playoffs three times—twice with the Montreal Canadiens and once with the Avalanche. He was a cool and fearless competitor. Some believe he was the best goalie in NHL history.

ADAM FOOTE   Defenseman

• BORN: 7/10/1971

• PLAYED FOR TEAM: 1991–92 TO 2003–04
  & 2007–08 TO PRESENT

Opponents who wanted to attack the Colorado net had to go through Adam Foote first. He was a clever and powerful skater who never backed down from a challenge. Foote loved to block shots and throw hard checks.

PETER FORSBERG   Center

- BORN: 7/20/1973 • PLAYED FOR TEAM: 1994–95 TO 2003–04 & 2007–08

Fans knew Peter Forsberg was a great scorer when he won the Calder Trophy as the league's best rookie. In the years that followed, he showed he could be a star at both ends of the ice. "Peter the Great" was a strong, smart defensive center and also an excellent passer and shooter.

MILAN HEJDUK   Right Wing

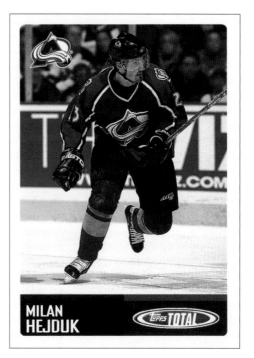

- BORN: 2/14/1976

- FIRST SEASON WITH TEAM: 1998–99

Milan Hejduk was a gifted goal scorer. He had a quick wrist shot and a sneaky backhand. The "Duke" led the NHL with 50 goals in 2002–03.

PAUL STASTNY   Center

- BORN: 12/27/1985

- FIRST SEASON WITH TEAM: 2006–07

The Avalanche proved that family matters when they drafted Paul Stastny, the son of Peter Stastny. Paul made his mark as one of the NHL's best passers. In 2007, he set a league record for rookies by scoring at least one point in 20 games in a row.

LEFT: Adam Foote
ABOVE: Milan Hejduk

Behind the Bench

In the early years of the World Hockey Association, many teams hired famous NHL players to coach them. They hoped these heroes would attract new fans. Two of Quebec's coaches were Maurice "Rocket" Richard and Jacques Plante. Both had been beloved stars for the Montreal Canadiens. Richard was the Nordiques' first coach, but he changed his mind at the beginning of the season and quit after two games!

The first coach to lead Quebec to the WHA Finals was Jean-Guy "Smitty" Gendron. He had been the team's captain as a player. Two years later, in 1976–77, Marc Boileau coached Quebec to the WHA championship. Quebec's most popular coach was Michel Bergeron. He built a high-scoring team during the 1980s.

In 1994, Marc Crawford became Quebec's coach. He won the Jack Adams Award as the NHL's top coach in his first season. A year later, Crawford was behind the bench in Colorado for the team's first Stanley Cup. In 1998, Bob Hartley took over the Avalanche. He led the team to the Stanley Cup in 2000–01.

Bob Hartley makes a point to his players during a 2001–02 game.

One Great Day

Few events in sports can match the action and excitement of Game 7 in the Stanley Cup Finals. Fans of the Avalanche know this better than anyone. Colorado faced the New Jersey Devils in the deciding game of the 2001 playoffs after a **shutout** by Patrick Roy in Game 6. The Avs hoped to win a "do-or-die" contest at home.

Early in the game, it was clear that Roy was still on a roll. The Devils didn't come close to scoring a goal. The Avs moved ahead in the first period on a great shot by Alex Tanguay. Early in the second period, Adam Foote banged a pass off the boards to Joe Sakic, who swooped in on the New Jersey goal. Martin Brodeur stopped his shot, but the rebound went right to Tanguay. He fired the puck into the unguarded net for a 2–0 lead.

Later in the period, Sakic gave Colorado a 3–0 lead with a goal from close range. His shot was a work of art. It went between a defenseman's skates and then rose over Brodeur's glove and into the upper right-hand corner of the net. The Devils finally scored in the second period, but it was too little too late. The Avalanche won, 3–1.

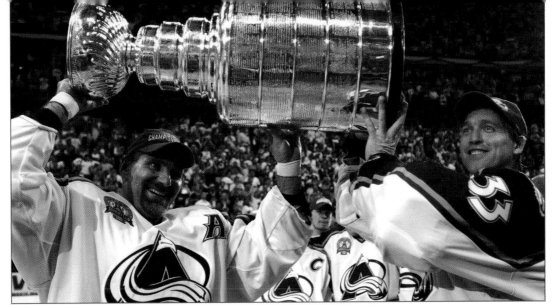

Ray Bourque and Patrick Roy lift the Stanley Cup after Game 7 in 2000–01.

After the game, Sakic was handed the Stanley Cup. He immediately gave it to Ray Bourque, who had waited more than 20 years for this moment. Bourque lifted the Cup above his head before kissing it twice. "After what he has accomplished in his career," Sakic said later, "he is the one who deserved to lift it first."

With two goals and an assist, Tanguay became the youngest player ever to get three points in Game 7 of the finals. Roy, meanwhile, became a Stanley Cup winner in a third *decade*. He had already captured the trophy with the Montreal Canadiens in 1986 and 1993, and with the Avs in 1996.

"For a little boy from Quebec, I never thought that would happen," Roy said. "It is not as special, to be honest with you, as seeing Ray raising that Cup in the middle of the ice, seeing his eyes, how excited he was. There is nothing better than winning."

Legend Has It

Which Colorado player had his name misspelled on the Stanley Cup?

LEGEND HAS IT that Adam Deadmarsh did. After helping the Avs win the Stanley Cup in 1996, Deadmarsh was amazed to see his last name etched into the trophy as "Deadmarch." It was not the first time a name had been spelled incorrectly on the Stanley Cup, but later it became the first misspelling that the NHL corrected.

Has an NHL team retired the number of a player who never played for them?

LEGEND HAS IT that the Nordiques did. In 1979, Quebec joined the NHL after the WHA went out of business. That first year, the Nordiques retired the number of J.C. Tremblay. There was only one problem: Tremblay had retired after seven seasons in Quebec. He never actually played for the team in an NHL game.

Who was the NHL's toughest goalie?

LEGEND HAS IT that Patrick Roy was. Starting in the 1990s, the Avalanche and the Detroit Red Wings had a red-hot rivalry. Many times, the two teams dropped their gloves and got into fights. Normally, goalies stay put when their teammates begin pushing and shoving—it's hard to "mix it up" wearing all that heavy equipment. But Roy liked to wander from his net. He had some *legendary* scuffles with Detroit goalies Chris Osgood and Mike Vernon.

LEFT: Adam Deadmarsh shows the correct spelling of his name.
ABOVE: A poster of J.C. Tremblay from his days in Quebec.

It Really Happened

In hockey, weak teams are supposed to get stronger through the draft. That's just what the Avalanche did—only in a weird new way. In 1991, when the team was still in Quebec, it had the worst record in the NHL. That meant the Nordiques had the first pick in the draft. The best player in **junior hockey** was Eric Lindros. Some said he could have played as a pro at age 16.

The Nordiques wanted Lindros, but he didn't want them. Lindros told the team that he would not play in Quebec City. For a time, hockey fans wondered what would happen. Would the NHL punish Lindros? Would the Nordiques waste their pick on a player who would rather sit than skate?

The Nordiques figured out a good plan. They decided to take Lindros in the draft and then trade him. They asked a very high price. The Philadelphia Flyers and New York Rangers both agreed to meet Quebec's demands. For a time, both teams thought they had made a deal for the young star. Much confusion and excitement followed. Finally, the Nordiques took Philadelphia's offer.

In exchange for Lindros, the Nordiques received draft picks, players, and money. When all was said and done, they ended up with

Peter Forsberg holds up the Stanley Cup in the spring of 2001.
It was his second championship with the Avs.

Peter Forsberg, Mike Ricci, Chris Simon, Ron Hextall, Jocelyn Thibault, Steve Duchesne, and Kerry Huffman. In one unbelievable trade, Quebec went from one of the worst teams in the NHL to one of the best. Four seasons later, after the Nordiques moved to Colorado, they were crowned NHL champions.

Team Spirit

Few hockey teams can say their fans are more loyal than Colorado's. After moving from Quebec in 1995–96, the Avalanche began selling out game after game after game. That season, in fact, the Avs started a streak in which they sold out all of their tickets for 487 games in a row. No NHL team has ever had a longer sellout streak.

Fans lucky enough to get tickets for those games were treated to one of the league's strangest **mascots**, Howler the Yeti. Yetis are legendary snow monsters, similar to Bigfoot. Howler had a big, furry head, a wide smile, and wore a hockey helmet.

In 2009, the team decided to create a new mascot named Bernie. He is a St. Bernard, a dog that is famous for rescuing skiers and mountain climbers stranded in deep snow. Bernie wears a Colorado jersey with the number one on the back. The number is actually a dog bone.

Bernie knows how to get Avalanche fans excited.

Timeline

The hockey season is played from October through June. That means each season takes place at the end of one year and the beginning of the next. In this timeline, the accomplishments of the Avalanche are shown by season.

1976–77
Quebec wins the WHA championship.

1991–92
The Nordiques trade for Peter Forsberg.

1972–73
The Nordiques play their first season in the WHA.

1979–80
The team joins the NHL.

1995–96
The team moves to Colorado and wins the Stanley Cup.

A bumper sticker celebrating Colorado's first Stanley Cup title.

Patrick Roy makes a save during the 2001–02 season.

2001–02
Patrick Roy is a First-Team NHL **All-Star**.

2006–07
Paul Stastny sets a rookie record with a point in 20 games in a row.

2000–01
The Avalanche win their second Stanley Cup.

2002–03
Milan Hejduk leads the NHL with 50 goals.

2008–09
Joe Sakic plays his final season.

Paul Stastny and Milan Hejduk

Fun Facts

DO YOU SMELL THAT, TOO?

When the Avalanche won their second Stanley Cup in 2001, left wing Shjon Podein didn't take off his uniform for more than 24 hours. "My dog didn't mind the smell, but my wife thought it was disgusting," he said.

THE 700 CLUB

When Patrick Roy retired from hockey in 2003, he held the record for most victories in the regular season plus playoffs (702). In 2009–10, goalie Martin Brodeur joined Roy as the only members of the NHL's "700 Club."

SECOND LANGUAGE

Although Joe Sakic grew up in Canada, he did not speak English as a young child. Instead he spoke Croatian, the language of his parents.

LIKE FATHER, LIKE SON

In 2006–07, Paul Stastny set a Colorado record for points by a rookie, with 51. Who holds the Quebec record? Paul's father, Peter, who had 109 points in 1980–81.

OH, BROTHER!

In a 1981 game, Peter and Anton Stastny combined for seven goals and nine assists.

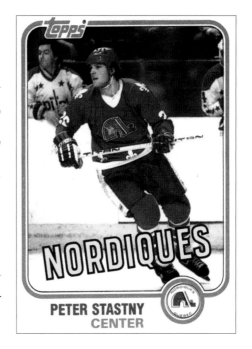

PETER STASTNY
CENTER

THE REAL DEAL

In Quebec's first NHL game, Réal Cloutier scored three times. Only two other players in league history had recorded a **hat trick** in their first NHL game.

TRIPLE TROUBLE

Five Avalanche players—Joe Sakic, Rob Blake, Alexei Gusarov, Valeri Kamensky, and Peter Forsberg—have won the Stanley Cup, a gold medal in the *Olympics*, and a World Championship. That makes them all members of the "triple gold club."

LEFT: Shjon Podein
ABOVE: Peter Stastny

Talking Hockey

"On the ice, Peter was the guy that made things go."

—Jamie Hislop, on high-scoring Peter Stastny

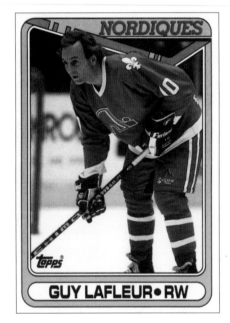

GUY LAFLEUR • RW

"It's with an enormous amount of pleasure that I return … I'd like to end my career in Quebec, where it began."

—Guy Lafleur, on playing his last professional season where he grew up as a boy

"When you stop playing and stop working hard, that's when the other team is going to be all over you the whole time."

—Peter Forsberg, on skating hard until the game is over

"I play a position where you make mistakes. The only people who don't make them at a hockey game are the ones watching."

—Patrick Roy, on the pressure to be perfect when defending the goal

ABOVE: Guy Lafleur
RIGHT: Marc Crawford

"You want to give the guys a framework that allows them to use their own creativity."
—*Marc Crawford, on how to get the most out of great players*

"You have justified the loyalty and pride of some **ferociously** loyal and proud fans."
—*President Bill Clinton, on the Avalanche's first Stanley Cup, in 1996*

"I told him we were going to win, and I wanted him to be the first one to lift it [the Stanley Cup]."
—*Joe Sakic, on the promise he made to Ray Bourque before the 2000–01 season*

"No feeling is better than this!"
—*Alex Tanguay, on scoring the goal that won the 2001 Stanley Cup*

For the Record

The great Quebec and Colorado teams and players have left their marks on the record books. These are the "best of the best" …

Peter Forsberg

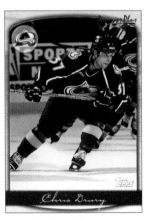

Chris Drury

AVALANCHE AWARD WINNERS

CALDER TROPHY
TOP ROOKIE

Peter Stastny	1980–81
Peter Forsberg	1994–95
Chris Drury	1998–99

HART MEMORIAL TROPHY
MOST VALUABLE PLAYER

Joe Sakic	2000–01
Peter Forsberg	2002–03

LADY BYNG MEMORIAL TROPHY
SPORTSMANSHIP

Joe Sakic	2000–01

ART ROSS TROPHY
TOP SCORER

Peter Forsberg	2002–03

CONN SMYTHE TROPHY
MVP DURING PLAYOFFS

Joe Sakic	1995–96
Patrick Roy	2000–01

MAURICE "ROCKET" RICHARD TROPHY
LEADING GOAL SCORER

Milan Hejduk	2002–03

ALL-STAR GAME MVP

Joe Sakic	2003–04

WHA MVP*

Marc Tardif	1975–76
Marc Tardif	1977–78

WHA ALL-STAR GAME MVP

Rejean Houle	1974–75
Réal Cloutier**	1975–76
Marc Tardif**	1977–78

WHA PLAYOFF MVP

Serge Bernier	1976–77

DENNIS A. MURPHY TROPHY
WHA BEST DEFENSEMAN

J.C. Tremblay	1972–73
J.C. Tremblay	1974–75

BILL HUNTER TROPHY
WHA SCORING LEADER

Marc Tardif	1975–76
Réal Cloutier	1976–77
Marc Tardif	1977–78
Réal Cloutier	1978–79

* *Known as the Gary Davidson Award & Gordie Howe Trophy.*

** *Shared this award with another player.*

AVALANCHE ACHIEVEMENTS

ACHIEVEMENT	YEAR
WHA Finalists	1974–75
WHA Champions	1976–77
Stanley Cup Champions	1995–96
Stanley Cup Champions	2000–01

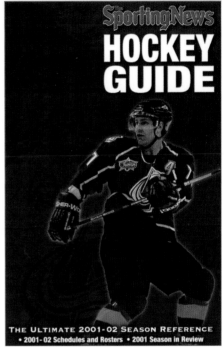

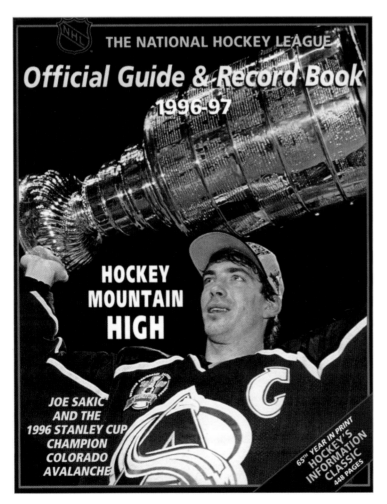

ABOVE: Ray Bourque appears on the cover of the *Sporting News Hockey Guide* after Colorado's 2000–01 championship.

LEFT: Joe Sakic is the cover boy on the NHL's *Official Guide & Record Book* for the 1996–97 season.

Pinpoints

T he history of a hockey team is made up of many smaller stories. These stories take place all over the map—not just in the city a team calls "home." Match the pushpins on these maps to the Team Facts and you will begin to see the story of the Avalanche unfold!

TEAM FACTS

1   Quebec City, Quebec, Canada—*The team played here as the Nordiques for 23 years.*

2   Denver, Colorado—*The Avalanche have played here since 1995–96.*

3   Rochester, Minnesota—*Shjon Podein was born here.*

4   Trumbull, Connecticut—*Chris Drury was born here.*

5   Burnaby, British Columbia, Canada—*Joe Sakic was born here.*

6   Toronto, Ontario, Canada—*Adam Foote was born here.*

7   Montreal, Quebec, Canada—*Ray Bourque was born here.*

8   Simcoe, Ontario, Canada—*Rob Blake was born here.*

9   Bratislava, Slovakia—*Peter, Anton, and Marian Stastny were born here.*

10 Usti nad Labem, Czech Republic—*Milan Hejduk was born here.*

11 Voskresensk, Russia—*Valeri Kamensky was born here.*

12 Belfast, Northern Ireland—*Owen Nolan was born here.*

Valeri Kamensky

Faceoff

Hockey is played between two teams of six skaters. Each team has a goalie, two defensemen, and a forward line that includes a left wing, right wing and center. The goalie's job is to stop the puck from crossing the red goal line. A hockey goal is six feet wide and four feet high. The hockey puck is a round disk made of hard rubber. It weighs approximately six ounces.

During a game, players skate as hard as they can for a full "shift." When they get tired, they take a seat on the bench, and a new group jumps off the bench and over the boards to take their place. Forwards play together in set groups, or "lines," and defensemen do too.

There are rules that prevent players from injuring or interfering with opponents. However, players are allowed to bump, or "check," each other when they battle for the puck. Because hockey is a fast game played by strong athletes, sometimes checks can be rough!

If a player breaks a rule, a penalty is called by the referee. For most penalties, the player must sit in the penalty box for two minutes. This gives the other team a one-skater advantage, or "power play." The team down a skater is said to be "short-handed."

NHL games have three 20-minute periods—60 minutes in all—and the team that scores the most goals when time has run out is the winner. If the score is tied, the teams play an overtime period. The first team to score during overtime wins. If the game is still tied, then it is decided by a shootout—a one-on-one contest between the goalies and the best shooters. During the Stanley Cup playoffs, no shootouts are held. The teams play until the tie is broken.

Things happen so quickly in hockey that it is easy to overlook set plays. The next time you watch a game, see if you can spot these plays:

PLAY LIST

DEFLECTION—Sometimes a shooter does not try to score a goal. Instead, he aims his shot so that a teammate can touch the puck with his stick and suddenly change its direction. If the goalie is moving to stop the first shot, he may be unable to adjust to the "deflection."

GIVE-AND-GO—When a skater is closely guarded and cannot get an open shot, he sometimes passes to a teammate with the idea of getting a return pass in better position to shoot. The "give-and-go" works when the defender turns to follow the pass and loses track of his man. By the time he recovers, it is too late.

ONE-TIMER—When a player receives a pass, he must control the puck and position himself for a shot. This gives the defense a chance to react. Some players are skilled enough to shoot the instant a pass arrives for a "one-timer." A well-aimed one-timer is almost impossible to stop.

PULLING THE GOALIE—Sometimes in the final moments of a game, the team that is behind will try a risky play. To gain an extra skater, the team will pull the goalie out of the game and replace him with a center, wing, or defenseman. This gives the team a better chance to score. It also leaves the goal unprotected and allows the opponent to score an "empty-net goal."

Glossary

HOCKEY WORDS TO KNOW

ALL-STAR—An award given to the league's best players at the end of each season.

ALL-STAR GAME—The annual game featuring the NHL's best players. Prior to 1967, the game was played at the beginning of the season between the league champion and an All-Star squad. Today it is played during the season. The game doesn't count in the standings.

ASSISTS—Passes that lead to a goal.

DIVISION—A group of teams that play in the same region.

DRAFTED—Chosen from a group of the best junior hockey, college, and international players. The NHL draft is held each summer.

EASTERN CONFERENCE FINALS—The series that determines which team from the East will face the best team from the West in the Stanley Cup Finals.

HAT TRICK—Three goals in one game.

JUNIOR HOCKEY—Leagues for young players who are not yet ready for the NHL.

LINEUP—The list of players who are playing in a game.

MOST VALUABLE PLAYER (MVP)—The award given each year to the league's best player; also given to the best player in the playoffs and All-Star Game.

NATIONAL HOCKEY LEAGUE (NHL)—The league that began play in 1917–18 and is still in existence today.

OVERTIME—The extra 20-minute period played when a game is tied after 60 minutes. Teams continue playing overtime periods until one team scores a goal and wins.

PLAYMAKER—A player who creates scoring opportunities.

PLAYOFFS—The games played after the season to determine the league champion.

PROFESSIONALS—Players that play a sport for money.

ROOKIE—A player in his first season.

SHUTOUT—A game in which a team is prevented from scoring.

STANLEY CUP—The championship trophy of North American hockey since 1893, and of the NHL since 1927.

STANLEY CUP FINALS—The series that determines the NHL champion each season. It has been a best-of-seven series since 1939.

VETERANS—Players with great experience.

WHA FINALS—The series that determined the WHA champion each season.

WORLD HOCKEY ASSOCIATION (WHA)—A rival league to the NHL that played from 1972–73 to 1978–79. When the WHA went out of business, four of its teams joined the NHL.

OTHER WORDS TO KNOW

ASSEMBLE—Put together.

DECADE—A period of 10 years; also specific periods, such as the 1950s.

DEMOCRATIC NATIONAL CONVENTION—The meeting at which the Democratic Party nominates a candidate for president of the United States.

ELUDED—Stayed out of reach.

ERA—A period of time in history.

FEROCIOUSLY—Extremely intense or devoted.

LEGENDARY—Famous.

LOGO—A symbol or design that represents a company or team.

MASCOTS—Animals or people believed to bring a group good luck.

OLYMPICS—An international sports competition held every four years.

PROVINCE—A specific region of a country.

REMARKABLE—Unusual or exceptional.

RIVALRY—Extremely emotional competition.

SYMBOL—Something that represents a thought or idea.

SYNTHETIC—Made in a laboratory, not in nature.

Places to Go

ON THE ROAD

COLORADO AVALANCHE
1000 Chopper Circle
Denver, Colorado 80204
(303) 405-1100

THE HOCKEY HALL OF FAME
Brookfield Place
30 Yonge Street
Toronto, Ontario, Canada   M5E 1X8
(416) 360-7765

ON THE WEB

THE NATIONAL HOCKEY LEAGUE   www.nhl.com
- *Learn more about the National Hockey League*

THE COLORADO AVALANCHE   avalanche.nhl.com
- *Learn more about the Avalanche*

THE HOCKEY HALL OF FAME   www.hhof.com
- *Learn more about hockey's greatest players*

ON THE BOOKSHELF

To learn more about the sport of hockey, look for these books at your library or bookstore:

- Keltie, Thomas. *Inside Hockey! The legends, facts, and feats that made the game.* Toronto, Ontario, Canada: Maple Tree Press, 2008.

- MacDonald, James. *Hockey Skills: How to Play Like a Pro.* Berkeley Heights, New Jersey: Enslow Elementary, 2009.

- Stewart, Mark and Kennedy, Mike. *Score! The action and artistry of hockey's magnificent moment.* Minneapolis, Minnesota: Lerner Publishing Group, 2010.

47

Index

PAGE NUMBERS IN **BOLD** REFER TO ILLUSTRATIONS.

The Team

MARK STEWART has written over 200 books for kids—and more than a dozen books on hockey, including a history of the Stanley Cup. He grew up in New York City during the 1960s and followed fun teams like the Nordiques after the WHA began in the 1970s. Mark shares the same July 7 birthday with Joe Sakic, and was one of the first writers to profile Sakic for young hockey fans, back in 1994. Mark comes from a family of writers. His grandfather was Sunday Editor of *The New York Times* and his mother was Articles Editor of *Ladies' Home Journal* and *McCall's*, and also wrote for *Sports Illustrated*. Mark has profiled hundreds of athletes over the last 20 years. He has also written several books about New York and New Jersey. Mark is a graduate of Duke University, with a degree in History. He lives with his daughters and wife Sarah overlooking Sandy Hook, New Jersey.

DENIS GIBBONS is a former newsletter editor of the Toronto-based Society for International Hockey Research (SIHR) and a writer and editor with *The Hockey News*. He was a contributing writer to the publication *Kings of the Ice: A History of World Hockey* and has worked as chief hockey researcher at six Winter Olympics for the ABC, CBS, and NBC television networks. Denis also has worked as a researcher for the FOX Sports Network during the Stanley Cup playoffs. He resides in Burlington, Ontario, Canada with his wife Chris.